GET OUT ALIVE!

ESCAPE FROM A DEADLY HUG

Julie K. Lundgren

Published in the United States of America by Cherry Lake Publishing Group
Ann Arbor, Michigan
www.cherrylakepublishing.com

Reading Adviser: Beth Walker Gambro, MS, Ed., Reading Consultant, Yorkville, IL

Photo Credits:
© Agus_Gatam/Shutterstock cover, contents page (python), page 9 (bottom), and page 22 (bottom); © Serenity Images23/Shutterstock cover (meerkats); © fiestachka/Shutterstock (graphic on cover and throughout book); © Cassette Bleue/Shutterstock, speech bubbles throughout; © Nazarkru/Shutterstock, yellow bursts throughout; © Gulliver20/Shutterstock page 4; © Heiko Kiera/Shutterstock (top); © Girish HC/Shutterstock page 5; © CGN089/Shutterstock, © hyotographics/Shutterstock (map) page 6; © Ramod Sunar/Shutterstock (top), Paul Tessier/Shutterstock page 7; © Padodo/Shutterstock page 8; © Patrick K. Campbell/Shutterstock (top), © Kurit afshen/Shutterstock pages 10 and 11; © irin-k/Shutterstock page 12; © Peter Hermes Furian/Shutterstock (map), © Oleksandr Lysenko/Shutterstock page 13; © sirtravelalot/Shutterstock (top), © Eric Isselee/Shutterstock page 14-15, © Squeeb Creative/Shutterstock page 15 (top); © Krisda Ponchaipulltawee/Shutterstock (python), © fototoy/Shutterstock page 16; © M Rose/Shutterstock (bottom) page 17; © dwi putra stock/Shutterstock (python), Likanaris/Shutterstock (sensor waves) page 18; © ANATOLY KOVTUN/Shutterstock page 19; © Maslov Dmitry/Shutterstock page 20; © NeagoneFo/Shutterstock (top), © FJAH/Shutterstock page 21; © Jesus Cobaleda/Shutterstock (top) page 22; © MP cz/Shutterstock page 23.

Produced for Cherry Lake Publishing by bluedooreducation.com

Copyright © 2026 by Cherry Lake Publishing Group

All rights reserved. No part of this book may be reproduced or utilized in any form or by any means without written permission from the publisher.

Library of Congress Cataloging-in-Publication Data has been filed and is available at catalog.loc.gov.

Printed in the United States of America

Note from Publisher: Websites change regularly, and their future contents are outside of our control. Supervise children when conducting any recommended online searches for extended learning opportunities.

About the Author

Julie K. Lundgren grew up in northern Minnesota near Lake Superior. She delighted in picking berries, finding cool rocks, and trekking in the woods. She still does! Julie's interest in nature science led her to a degree in biology. She adores her family, her sweet cat, and Adventure Days.

Contents

WOULD YOU LIKE A HUG? 4
I AM A SUPER PREDATOR! 8
SMART CLIMBERS 12
GET OUT ALIVE! 16
FIND OUT MORE 24
GLOSSARY 24
INDEX 24

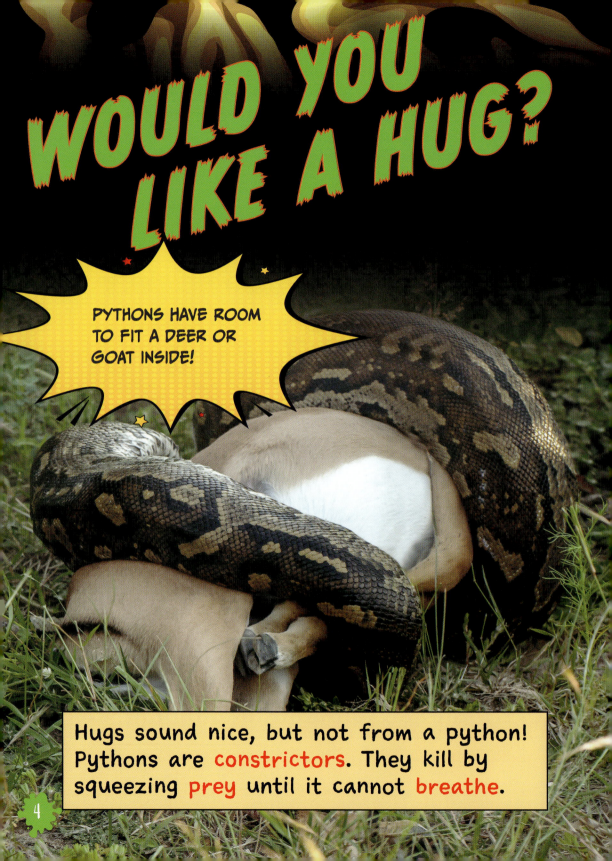

WOULD YOU LIKE A HUG?

PYTHONS HAVE ROOM TO FIT A DEER OR GOAT INSIDE!

Hugs sound nice, but not from a python! Pythons are constrictors. They kill by squeezing prey until it cannot breathe.

4

Burmese pythons live in Southeast Asia. Pet pythons have escaped and survived in the United States. Thousands of them live in southeastern places now!

THEIR NAME COMES FROM A COUNTRY ONCE CALLED BURMA. IT IS NOW MYANMAR.

Like other reptiles, pythons get heat from the sun, air, and land around them. They cannot live where it is cold.

BURMESE PYTHONS CAN LAY UP TO 100 EGGS AT A TIME.

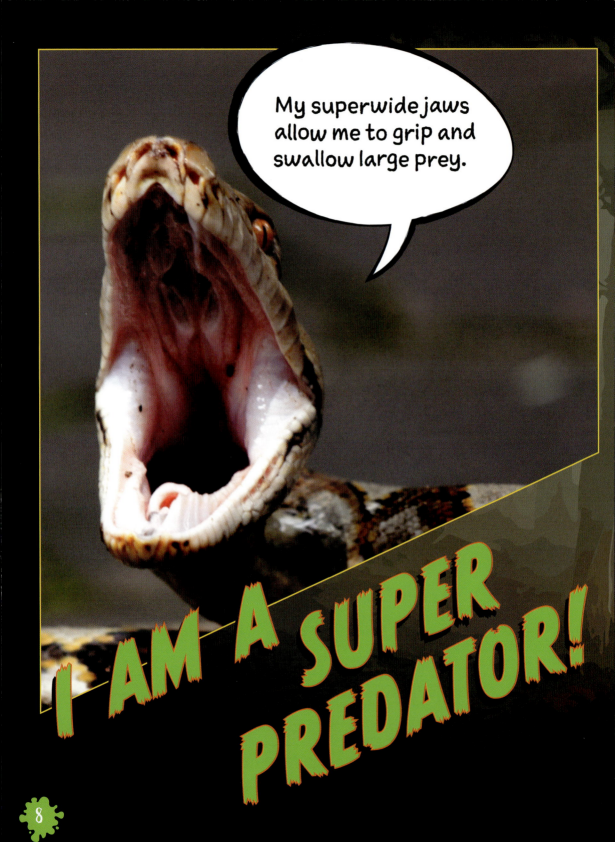

COLORFUL, PATTERNED SKIN HELPS BURMESE PYTHONS BLEND INTO DRY LEAVES AND GRASSES.

TO FIND PREY IN THE DARK, THEY TASTE THE AIR WITH THEIR TONGUES. THEY ALSO USE **HEAT SENSORS** IN THEIR JAWS.

Pythons rely on speed and sneak attacks. Their teeth catch and grip their prey. Then they wrap around it in a deadly hug.

IN SOUTHEAST ASIA, BURMESE PYTHONS MAY EAT LEOPARDS AND ANTELOPES. IN THE U.S., THEY MAY EAT ALLIGATORS AND BOBCATS!

Pythons squeeze tighter each time their prey breathes out. The snakes coil tighter and tighter until the prey suffocates.

BURMESE PYTHONS EAT BIRDS, RATS, FROGS, AND LARGER ANIMALS.

SMART CLIMBERS

Meet one of the Burmese python's favorite foods, the black rat. Also called house rat or ship rat, it often lives near people.

Black rats are most active at night. Their eyes, ears, nose, and whiskers help guide them to food and detect danger in the dark.

A rat's front teeth grow its entire life. Rats chew on wood, bark, or other hard material to keep their teeth sharp and trim.

BLACK RATS USE THEIR LONG TAILS FOR BALANCE WHEN THEY CLIMB.

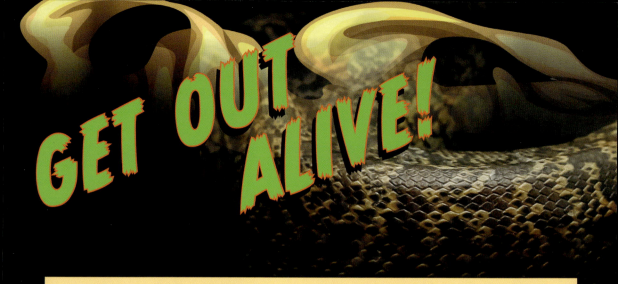

GET OUT ALIVE!

In the warm night, a large Burmese python slithers along the ground. Its tongue flicks to taste the air. It detects a black rat nearby!

A black rat has left its cozy nest and family to find food. It sniffs out some tasty seeds.

RATS LIVE IN GROUPS FOR THE BEST CHANCE OF SURVIVAL.

The python's head turns from side to side, finding its target.

As it eats, the rat hears rustles in the grass. Is it the wind—or possible death?

The black rat rises on its hind legs, teeth showing. Those teeth are no match for the huge snake!

The giant snake moves on, still hungry. It will find other food tonight.

Find Out More

Books

Ciletti, Barbara. *Burmese Pythons*, Mankato, MN: Black Rabbit Books, 2017

Hansen, Grace. *Rats*, Minneapolis, MN: Abdo Publishing, 2017

Websites

Search these online sources with an adult:

Rats | National Geographic Kids

Burmese Pythons | Animal Fact Guide

Glossary

breathe (BREETH) move air into and out of one's lungs

constrictors (kuhn-STRIK-terz) snakes that squeeze their prey to death

detect (dee-TEKT) find and identify, often using the body's senses

heat sensors (HEET SEN-surz) special skin organs on snakes' heads that allow them to detect the body heat of prey

prey (PRAY) animals hunted and eaten by other animals

rustles (RUS-uhlz) light swishing sounds

suffocates (SUF-uh-kayts) dies from lack of air or breathing

tongue (TUNG) mouthpart for sensing taste

tropical (TROP-uh-kuhl) warm and moist year round

Index

climb(ing) 14, 15
eggs 7
food(s) 12, 13, 16
jaws 8, 9

nose 13
prey 4, 8, 9, 10, 11
seeds 16
squeeze 11, 21

tail(s) 5, 15
teeth 10, 15, 20
tongue(s) 5, 9, 16